In All Their Animal Brilliance

Poems by

LANCE LARSEN

UNIVERSITY OF TAMPA PRESS • TAMPA, FLORIDA

Manufactured in the United States of America
Printed on acid-free paper ∞
First Edition

The University of Tampa Press
401 West Kennedy Boulevard
Tampa, FL 33606

ISBN 1-879852-31-4 (cloth)
ISBN 1-879852-32-2 (pbk.)

Browse & order online at

http://utpress.ut.edu

Larsen, Lance, 1961-
   In all their animal brilliance : poems / by Lance Larsen.-- 1st ed.
      p. cm.
   ISBN 1-879852-31-4 (cloth : alk. paper) -- ISBN 1-879852-32-2 (pbk : alk. paper)
   I. Title.
   PS3562.A738I5 2004
   811'.54--dc22   2004025107

CONTENTS

III. Shadow and Trace

IV. Stations of the Sky

For Jacqui, once again

We both believe, and disbelieve a hundred times an Hour, which keeps Believing nimble.

– Emily Dickinson

Short Allegory, with Mirrors

If I goggled my hands around my eyes just right
and pressed my face straight into that wall

of kindergarten mirrors, like Narcissus trying
to enter his own stillness, I found not a silver river,

but an observation room. Inside that delicious
dark, a trinity of co-eds was taking notes

about me—did I share properly, were my wrists
wired to evil birds, what parables of sadness flew

from my mouth? They had girl adult bodies,
those watchers, and shook their beautiful heads

no and no, then pointed me with their chewed
pencils back into the lying sunlight of this world.

I. Landscape for Several Pairs of Hands

Platonic

They smelled like gristle and lost rivers, those talons.
I wore them around my neck
on fishing line.
They guarded that palace behind my breastbone
where the soul takes its R & R.

What creatures that pair of legs perished into.
Pull the tendons, and the talons
preached. Opening
and closing like a glad
maniac deciding between death by snakebite

and death by voodoo.
And when the talons gripped my finger
till it purpled I felt
great wings feather the air,
straining to pull me out of my body.

Black Box

You enter as a mother on a bus, exit a blade of grass.
Enter as a shoe shiner, leave as a fetlock
on a draft horse, or a spider riding
that fetlock toward a leaning barn.
You become the thing you didn't know you needed.
A crow wing left under a tree.
A chipped marble a second grader hides
in her mouth during reading time.
Transformation is not a place.
Begin with loose change, or a staticky song, fold
in a little rain, and end up a boy
climbing stairs into a sky on fire.
Or a woman surprised by the smallness of her body.
Let weather or a P.S. be the black box—
or a bus ride. Once you step off,
convert the alley of sleeping cats into a path.
Learn to walk without moving,
move without mistaking wind for progress.
Back home, Poland smolders
whether you open the atlas or leave it under the hungry
goldfish. You drink, but the water sloshes
through you, splashing your bones
all the way to the floor. Your task today: grow
a new throat. Your task: stare at a lake
or gutted car till your sister's eyes stare back.
I said black box, I said transformation.
I mean questions you crawl through when your life
stalls. I have left white space
at the end in case you need extra pauses in the middle.

This World, Not the Next

True, God dreamed our first parents out
    of a chaos of firmament and longing.
And true, he pled with them to return
    to a savory Forever of his making.
But it was this world, with its tides and machinery
    of sweet decay, they learned to love.

He touched their hair, then covered their sleeping
    mouths with His and declared breath
holy, but forced them to draw another
    and another. He commanded that they eat
not of that dazzling tree of awe and penumbra,
    but knew its fruit would eat at them.

And when it did, and when they fell
    into knowing, God folded the garden and hid it
deep inside the woman, but commanded
    the man to tend it. And in due season the man
Eved, and the woman Adamed back
    and the song of radiance they keened was pure

darkness by morning. And God blessed
    their bounty to be infinite, but left them
ten crooked fingers to count with.
    And buried His echo inside their bodies,
a delicious lapping that answered *yes* and *yes*
    to a question neither could recall.

Winter Takeout

In the pass, fishtailing around corners, in the whiteout
of maybe and two-way traffic, I said *yes*

to everything. Yes to snow heavy as Ecclesiastes.
Yes to vertigo and the wheels locking up

if it came to that. Yes to the physics of forehead
kissing glass and the hush of more snow

and whatever follows clarity—being found clean
or found out. At the truck stop all I could manage

was hunger. So I ordered a catcher's mitt
of a cinnamon roll slathered in icing, and waited,

hunched at the counter, beside swinging kitchen doors.
That's when she sidestepped past, her hands

on my waist her only *excuse me*. A waitress in stripes
and the heavy blue of December mascara.

But releasing carefully, like a skater. Silly to call
that incident holy. Her hands didn't linger.

Her minced steps and the pout of her body
were only fatigue. But so what? I needed to be touched.

I could call her Casualene and say she looked
like her name only sadder. That all night I had felt

my ransomed body sliding along ice and barbed wire,
and felt it here needled by a scratchy jukebox.

I could say I licked my fingers all the way to Idaho.
All true. How I ached to guarantee her a charmed life.

How chivalric and beside the point I was.
How dark the highway, how much darker the snow.

Drainage Pipe Under I-89

When it was too hot to hunt scorpions or skinks
I practiced death. The same two hundred feet
of corrugated riddle each time, but a new
matrix of mosquito bites and peeling
sunburn across my back. Insert my head
and cancel the sky. Ease my shoulders
through and erase a subdivision of tanning
mothers doing crossword puzzles with God.
Ritual of cobweb and rat turd, scrape
of hand and opposite knee. I lay down
in that sweet mausoleum, and speeding
cars above took turns with my body.
And now I lay still, and now my spirit floated
from mourner to mourner, like a question
mark trying to complete a sentence.
Extra hovers over girls at the city pool
I had never touched, which was all of them.
And now I was the taste of a closed mouth
in a closed room. And now water,
wettest when it flows through dry waiting.
I had dirt for hair, my finger for a toothbrush.
A social security number that began
with 519 and ended where my legs used to be.
Indian paint brush, waterleaf, locoweed,
dogtooth violet. I said the names like ice
till the dead filled me. My three dead cats
squirmed in first, then my miscarried brother
dragging ghosts from the Eden inside my mother.
Then I was crawling through a midnight
exactly like the closed trunk of my cousin's

cherried-out GTO I climbed into once, at a drive-in,
on a dare, wondering when will the world click
open, when will I gather back into form?

On Thawing Her Milk

Two confessions, love. First, I always use the microwave
to thaw your milk, this morning included.
Second, I dreamed last night even *I* could breast feed.
A nurse floated me through a gauntlet of pregnant
women to a springy-haired o.b.—part Freud,
part ruddy John the Baptist. He inched
the stethoscope across my chest. *Yes,* he said,
sometimes fathers, if they have lucky genes and if
they complete the proper exercises and if they truly desire it . . .

I knew I wanted to be the child again—
did I now want to be the mother, as well?
Watching baby girl nurse yesterday,
she half asleep, and you slumped in the gauze
of late dusk, I thought, here is the purling
of lovers, only calmer and lazier.
And nothing at all like those breast-feeding
Renaissance Marys at the museum last week.
Always erect, those mothers—poised for history.

Never reclining or engorged, never rapturous.
Breasts too small and too perfectly suspended,
like props in a Ptolemaic science project.
Outside, blue irises. Inside, microwave beeping
again. I remove the bottle, shake it three times,
then take a quick taste for temperature.
Then a longer one. Why not? Baby girl
is content with my pinky in her mouth. And you—
you're miles away, and neither too cold nor too hot.

Walking on My Hands, Hotel Pool

Going under felt narcotic, like being dipped in blue
deafness, my road trip hair,
then my burned shoulders and torso.
It's what I needed that night:
to gather my body
from the horizons and plant
it somewhere specific,
to say *I* and mean *I*, to walk around
on the knotted hands I had gripped
the desert with through three barren states.

Ten years later, I want to say *I* and remember
the *world,* taste my life
that night from someone else's balcony.
A Thai waitress perhaps, touching
the countries tattooed across her husband's back
the evening he was paroled.
She looks down from some edge
of twilight. Looks down—
my milky legs cutting across water
not pointing at the moon but pedaling the sky.

Allegory, with Famous Poet

Make no mistake, the tangled beauty the boy hurries
through is a garden. Before he can scramble
away, before we can encumber him with a cowlick
and deformed eleventh toe, or pin on him
a profile ravaged by early repression, a window

opens. Call this rupture a second level in the poem.
Which makes the garden, with its affluence
of clematis and cat dung, a first level.
The boy looks up to a searing grammar of whiteness,
of which the woman herself is the principal verb.

She lowers a bowl and silver tray, the whole
contraption of knots and twine spinning crazily,
like a chivalrous plot. But who can say who
is rescuing whom? If we call this Amherst 1851,
and if we name the benefactress Emily, the boy's

predicament remains unchanged: wish for a piece
of gingerbread or a quatrain? I'm trying to keep erotics
out of this. I'm trying not to play the part
of the idling boy. But there's that constellation
of whiteness hanging above, birds jabbering in flight,

and the gilt tray like Jacob's ladder begging to serve
as commerce between. Does Emily request
a day lily? Does the boy instead sit on the tray
and lift his arms, thus asking to be taken up?
Is rapture a way to descend without condescending?

Walking home, the boy has no words for the worlds
dissolving in his mouth. Or in our mouths
if we have read with our bodies. When he looks back,
a dark window flashes questions he asks
by not asking. Whiteness is only sometimes a color.

Hand Poem

Poems lost inside hands lost inside poems.
It would be simpler to make
each finger a noun, and the skin syntax.
Easier, to let the hand like a good Buddhist
find its way by divine inattention.

This hand wears its verbs the way a corpse
wears stories, the way a lake wears
acres of brushed light.
That is, without much worry
about epistemology.

This hand would prefer to bury
itself in compost, or close on a duskier hand
across the street.
To trade fleshy secrets, like octopuses mating,
like sky marrying earth.

Poor thing—scarred, subsisting
on blood, marooned
at the end of a white and fastidious arm,
unable to declaim about
hands lost inside poems lost inside hands.

By Road and Sky

Hit and left for dead, this porcupine. A mess of flesh
and entrails in a smear of blood. It jerked a little,
then tried dragging itself away. My father pulled
over and rummaged in the trunk for something to finish
it off. My father was coolness that night. Or was he grace?
He straddled that twitching porcupine and raised
a tire iron above his head. I watched. Still it was my mother
I loved. My mother in the front seat, with her pill box hat
and apricot skirt. My mother, with a sleek armada
of moles above her collarbone and her left front tooth
overlapping the right. She turned away from the slash
of high beams across asphalt and the valley opening below.

I was not her first son, or favorite. But the one lucky
enough to ride in the backseat that night. The one whose face
she used as a mirror to watch my father rain down
six shivering blows. She reached for me across the seat,
then turned on the radio, as if I or the evening needed
serenading. The wedding reception we were late for
could wait. And the city juggling its neon promises.
And my father explaining that bad driving is to accidents
as a tire iron is to mercy. My mother held me. The ghost
of the porcupine hovered over its remains, then rose
with the moon and drifted south. And the road
said *never* and the sky said *always* and both told the truth.

Landscape, with Hungry Gulls

If I said *burial,* if I said *a lovely morning*
 to prepare the body, who would I startle?
Not this pair of teenage girls in matching swim suits
 making a mound of their brother.
And not the boy himself, laid out like a cadaver
 on rye, who volunteered for interment.

In the language of skin, he knows that sand rhymes
 with patience, and that patience worketh
a blue sky dotted with gulls, if only he remains
 still enough. And he does, his face a cameo
dusted with sparkling grains. Meanwhile, my son
 brings me offerings he has dug up—

a jaw bone, a pair of vertebrae, ribs like planks, three teeth.
 At my feet, an ancient horse assembles.
A lesson in calcification? A beginner's oracle kit?
 If the sea gulls canvassing the beach
are questions, then the pelican riding the dihedral breeze
 above the buoys is an admonition, but to what?

The sisters are at work again, making a giant
 Shasta daisy of their brother's face,
six pieces of popcorn per petal, his eyes blinking.
 Now they scatter leftover kernels across the mound
like sextons scattering lime. To my left,
 ankle deep in shallows, my son catches minnows.

No, not minnows, damsel fly larvae,
 which swim like minnows but have six legs.
He places them in a moat, so they can swim freely.

Soon enough they will climb this castle wall.
Soon enough they will shed their syntax
    and leave water for air, like a good translation.

The sisters move farther down the beach
    in hopes that the sea gulls will make a snack
of their brother. So many motives.
    Theirs: to dress a body in sand and stillness.
His: to sip the world, mouth to beak.
    The gulls draw closer, to peck at his heart.

I am pretending the body is only an idea.
    I watch the pelican. I keep reminding myself.
A pelican is not a pterodactyl with feathers.
    A pelican is not doing moral reconnaissance.
A pelican does not know my name.
    I close my eyes long enough to drift up and up.

Poor man, napping there far below, who looks
    and smells like me, but is stuck in a beach chair.
Quick, someone teach him to bank and hover.
    And this horse my son is decorating the moat with,
broken into pieces so various and eloquent—
    where are its pastures, does it have enough to eat?

Landscape for Several Pairs of Hands

No one is going to save me from the rest of my life,
though my father,
seat belted and ruddy, hands like a surgeon's,
believes otherwise. He drives
as if landscape were no more than a long stretch
of obedient patients. But this is Wyoming,
where even angels and barbed wire
wait till after midnight to carry out their Q and A's.

Between us, a bleached cow skull, a sepulcher
of a face—our only souvenir
after hunting arrowheads all morning
and peeing rivulets that branched and crossed,
crossed and branched.
Next spring and onward into a geologist's eternity,
my father will hang this skull
in the crotch of our cherry tree—a warning

to marauding robins. Which they will ignore.
I am not quite asleep,
but can already feel hands crescendoing
across the horizon, hands
playing tuneful mirages that quiet away
just as I'm about to recognize
a melody. When I wake up
I will occupy a stronger, but sadder body.

It is August, nobody's birthday.
I am cold enough in this shimmering heat
to know my days as a son
are numbered. My father's right palm
settles on the cow skull. I touch it too.
We have crossed the meandering
Green River three times in one hour,
although our unpaid-for car is aimed straight west.

II. In All Their Animal Brilliance

Good Friday

San Bernardo, Chile

First a wavery premonition, then their snouts
breaking through haze, finally a rumble
of shank and muscled fat. Was it patience
that filled their pig eyes? Awe that filled me?
Down the street they came, through a veil
of fog and taboo. Smartly hooved, faces
lifted, as if being unclean also made them saintly.

Seven of them, which I, on my way to buy
bread, had divided. Seven days, seven venial sins,
seven sacred holes in my unholy face, seven
times seventy the times I must wash in ashes
and kiss the gristle of this sweet dying earth,
seven heavens watching. And they trotted,
my tallness less to them than a pillar of salt.

Tarantula on the Back of My Wrist

I want my questions to pulse like a tarantula
above haired legs. I want to believe the soul spiders
through its detritus of days the way
a tarantula climbs. Now pausing. Now moving
in a light-footed silence, like sadness channeling
a dead composer. If not my sadness, then my father's.
It terrified me, the way he used to sleep. Flat
on his back, pillow over his face, as if night were a burial.

If God is watching this closet drama unfold
he has sent only the usual signs—
a snowy yard italicized by stars, a house settling
deeper into its footnotes.
I have no idea if the soul has a mouth.
If it does, surely it needs the body to taste the world.
I mean my arm holding up a spider.
I mean my father holding up a midnight full of questions.

Mr. Tarantula begins his soft shoe campaign again.
A pair of fangs, eight legs,
feelers like legs too, one leg half missing.
And me trying to translate that candor into time line
and caesura. I can't leave it alone,
this short leg that makes me wonder
how the soul wears its wounds.
This short leg that touches the world by not touching it.

Up ahead, where my sleeve begins he senses what,
a turn in the path, a dark place to hide?
Forgive me, Father,
for bringing you into this poem
without first waking you up. I said the soul,
but I mean the son inside me
following his mouth in search of hungers.
Where, sweet Jesus, is mercy in this analogy?

House Sit

It was like falling asleep to Chopsticks and waking
to Chopin, like taking a wrong turn
on your way to the fridge and ending
up in a painting by Zurbarán. All of it so easy—
abandon our pile of student things and coo
softly to their much nicer pile across town.
And guard their front door against the unwashed,
and wash the kitchen with wafts
of cut lemon, and lemonade our tired bodies
while watching sprinklers splash topiary swans.
Rilke was our everyday. Salvation Army
our sometimes. But for now we put on.
Put on cul-de-sacs and manicured sky.
Put on the thwonk thwonk of tennis across the moat,
the ecstatic Spanish of nannies.
And every evening we leashed ourselves
to the family hound, who zigzagged us
into an allegory of country club stinks.
Winston, they called him,
as if those Churchchillian eyes could erase
the nastiness he ferreted out with his nose.
Here the less-is-more of smashed squirrel,
there the zen of dung multiplied
by wind and summer flies. Could we learn it all?
Maids opened upstairs windows
to coax it in. Robins carried it from roof
to roof. And lizards on stucco walls converted
what was left into a mosaic of sleep.
We paused at a rummy apricot tree
and from its branches ate what no one else wanted.

Back in the borrowed house, we put on
a new nakedness. Which was often,
since the pool grew addicted to our student shoulders
and the gilded mirror watched us brush
our student teeth and the cat mewed for more
student hunger rising from what was never
a student bed. And shouldn't waking up feel
like a Bergman film translated into color?
And isn't the body a tangled garden no one can leave?

Old Masters

Like having harbingers inside my head.
More specifically magpies.
More specifically, magpies feathered
in radiant but dated tuxedos.
Magpies dancing
like St. Vitus, their gawky tails
signing *not flight, not song*
but this hopping way of staying hungry.

Salamander

Not one god under this smudged braille
 of newsprint in my window well, but two—
  braiding like a pair of naked teenagers.
 If in a previous life I slogged through marshes
to slaughter your loved ones, if I minced
  them and sold them in vials, if I was paid
   in cinnabar and a harvest moon rising
 above drunken fields, forgive me.
I touch you—wetter than adultery,
 cleaner than accident. Your gills are manifestos.
  I feel a delicious Me / Not Me
  debate rising up from the tiger stripes
of your skin. Mud puppies, cousins of fire,
 what secrets of the afterlife burn in your underlife?
  You are waiting for me to name you,
  but I do not know what you are.
Only what I am—a man who falls each morning
 into his same frightened breath.
  If I lifted you in my palm, like a compass,
  carried you in my mouth, the way
our first parents did, would your poisons sweeten
 my desire, could I slide through backyard
  pools, like water before it was water?

Spider Luck

One toe-nudge too many and she exploded, poor
mother spider, into a slick of babies—no more
than spilled commas, unless you knelt
at the open door with a paperback *Beowulf,*

as I did, to rescue them, and happened
to notice the pool playing *hide the button*
with Cassiopeia and wondered about heroic codes
in general and my cowardice in specific

for not swimming naked at 2:30 am and which lunatic
neighbor slipped into my apartment to steal
half a rotisseried chicken while I mailed a letter
and which one I should trust to water my ferns

and why rain is almost never a possessive
and whether I was the only one awake enough
to hear the wind saying with its hundred
mouths, *Never mind, little orphan, never mind.*

Not Pastoral

Not this road stitching together farms and gossipy
sheep and enough lyric mooning to erase
the Industrial Revolution. Not these maples gathered
creek side like aging land barons. And certainly not
these glazed hills—a Sunday painter's rapture,
the old-fashioned kind one does without body parts.

And please, not another cluster of mail boxes
pertly white, imitating an apple-pie childhood
no one had. Not this blissful sun or these fence posts,
and not this rented Buick, trunk so whispery clean
I'm ready to dig up a corpse or two and ferry
them around till the whole county stinks of death.

And not my smiling picnic of a face in the rear-view,
a mix-and-match affair resembling too many
mustached arsonists. These city eyes need blight.
Not more hollyhocks and ponds, not this pair
of barefoot girls tossing a Frisbee that wobbles orange
and translates both *flight* and *return* as *sky sky sky*.

Planaria

Run for a dictionary if you're the type that needs
a definition straight off.
But to learn *planaria* the way my brother did
you'll have to put on lug-soled boots
and carry two pounds of pig liver
into scrub oak. You'll have to hike for an hour
saying a prayer to the hog
that gave up his liver for science.

You'll have to hum something bluesy
to purge your blood of intention,
then whistle off-key to trick lost paths
into remembering your feet.
Planaria—take two steps for each of his,
the backs of his knees opening
and closing like baby mouths. *Planaria*—
kneel down to hook liver to a rusty lure.

And again *planaria*—splosh that slippery
bundle of blood into a stream.
We could have waited, but sometimes it's better
to give definitions and science projects
room to breathe. Better to unroll
sleeping bags blue as ghosts, better to feed
a fire with tinder true as stories.
When we returned, moon gleamed everywhere.

My brother lifted the liver from the stream.
Its blackness looked like the blackness
of before, but dripping with water.
Water and planaria. There—I've said it.
An order of related small soft-bodied free-living,
turbellarian flatworms moving
by means of cilia. See what I mean
about definitions? Squirmy as leeches, but smaller.

Planaria cannot see light. They grow fat on water
and blood. With mild shocks,
you can race them through a bath tub
slalom course. Cut them
just right, and they will grow an extra head.
That's what my brother lowered
into a coffee can and snapped the lid over.
He carried that squirming song through the dark.

When I couldn't stay warm that night,
my brother zipped our sleeping bags together
and we fell asleep counting
constellations we could point to but not name.
All night, the smell of fire kept oblivion
close. All night, to the left of our heads,
that coffee can—rock securing
its lid—failing to contain the word *planaria*.

Infinity Hopscotch

Poor dead stray—I gentle her ears, then wrap her in a towel
to soak up blood. Bury her beside my climbing rose.

No rain, but a sky bent on trying and a damp smell
midway between old suppers and penance.

Like a good citizen I try to walk under and through all this.
Which leads me to the sidewalk, and a newly chalked

hopscotch troll. She grins in pastels, electric and maternal,
the work of who knows which cul-de-sac imp.

From her pink scribbled hair, chalk circles big as plates,
patient as planets lead to the darkening orchard.

My shovel grows heavy—more hopping, more erasable
worlds, and no one to tell me when to change feet.

Yellowstone, Burning

As in pillars of devouring flames, as in honeymooners
driving west through pines fidgety as bridesmaids.
Fire is everywhere, the ranger said, but safely distant.
The radio gave us updates about wind
velocity and the new ecology of burning.
At an overlook, brush in hand, you hung
your hot hair over the railing,
as if the abyss below needed combing too.
Clouds of smoke drifted into next week
like leftover punctuation. When I replay smells,
plumy geysers drift in, spraying us
with a sulfury command to touch our secret parts
to the sky, to let the sky diagram our local fires.
A flock of blue-footed something flew up and away.
A papa buffalo nuzzled our car.
Even the antelopes, ricocheting through trees,
tried to warn us about being trapped in flesh.
You ate finger foods and lotioned your legs.
I read Rilke and a year-old *Newsweek* until I grew hungry
for the skin beneath your skin, the garden inside
the burning. Where was that country?
The whole afternoon turned *almost*. We almost swam
the Firehole River with those beautiful,
unshaved Spaniards. We almost joined the search
for a widow's lost poodle. We almost,
I swear, slipped out of our bodies into something slower
and deeper. Kiss me inside and out,
under, on top of. Such dizzy stanzas of smoke.

Legion

Imps of my childhood, left-handed guardians,
come back. You who led me each day
through a labyrinth of alleys and lunch lines,
dog crap and taboo, you who recorded
knock-knock jokes, state capitals, and the times
tables of lust in the same flesh, return.
I'm two car payments and enough exit ramps
of boredom past 35, to abhor respectable aging.

Where is the body I put on each morning,
gamy and bristling, skin itchy
with not knowing? Bluster me forward,
Saint Five Finger Discount. Shortcut me home,
Saint of Fattened Tick under my Arm
and Hallelujah. I'm willing to read the guts
of each squirrel I deadeyed from my window,
to let bloody robin feathers settle in my hair.

Rescue me like a botched science project,
let a folded gum wrapper and pee
complete the circuit and light the bulb.
Saint of Lost Sundays, show me again how to ride
cheap perfume and graceless hymns,
how to follow the breath back into the mouth
and be swallowed like a scab of bread.
Saint Why Not? Saint Says Who?

Saint Gravestone Seance under the Porcupine Tree—
I'm waiting for crawling and disdain
and a leap year holiday involving amputation.
Settle on nothing, but bring enough praying
mantises to green up the day. How many
magpies and bridges per cough? How many
caves in the sky? How long till you whisper
my name and I happily fall out of this face?

III. Shadow and Trace

On Being Asked, *Have you ever written about Jacqui's paintings?*

I've stolen three titles from her and so many shades
of blue that I gave up
and translated them all as *longing*.
You decide if that means yes or no.
Her hands, chipped nails and all, belonged to paint
long before I tried to belong to them.
Forgive me for getting mired in wanting

each canvas to turn into a room
in which she and I
try to erase each other's boundaries.
Think of chairs swimming around your head.
Of ferns dreaming of rain.
Of a glass table set for ghosts.
Does a hardwood frame make this a painting?

Does a story about the artist at twelve
dumpster diving for price tags the color of eels
make this a poem? I sit and I sit.
And desire in the shape of a husband passes through
this lush flatness like a piece of river wanting
to hold still by moving faster.
She calls this piece *Seven White Goldfish*.

Only none are white.
Only I count five and a half, not seven.
Paint is slow. Mouths even slower,
and hold only one word
at a time. The trick she said is keeping
the table empty enough
for God, whether you expect him for lunch or not.

Cottage Industry

On Sebastião Salgado's photograph "Outskirts of Guatemala City, 1978"

How many apples can a *campesina* carry on her head?
Assume she is six and a half, that each apple is sticky
with caramel, that her cardboard tray bends

but doesn't buckle. The girl, bottom left, a study
in doggedness and braided hair, threatens to walk
straight out of the frame. Meanwhile, from inside

a postage stamp of a window, top right, a woman
(the girl's mother?) watches. The planks
between them are weathered enough for pathos,

the woman's face a diagram in chiaroscuro and waiting,
so why insist on kinship? Isn't it enough to try,
and fail, to keep both faces in focus at once?

If the girl weren't bearing third-world innocence,
if the woman weren't pinned in place like a tin saint,
maybe we could shrug off the sheen of those apples,

five rows of four. Their sticks point everywhere,
like army compasses gone berserk—east is to west
as poverty is to always. And of course the apples

might not be carameled at all, but candied.
Who can say with black and white, which turns
even the simplest colors theoretical? I mean twenty

floating apples. I mean the one I singled out
to buy but can't. I mean the one the girl is eating
so casually, as if it were not money or her future.

On a Thumbprint in a Library Book

Thank you, whoever you are, for making a signature
out of blood, a red oasis in the margin.
Did an old wound open anew,
or did you cut yourself turning pages?
One pristine print, haloed by a smear of half prints.
Like a moon in its phases. Like a novelist
slipping into a wardrobe of minor characters.

Or like me, looking around this crosstown bus
trying on each face to keep me
from turning the page. We have all felt our lives
leaking into the world, all put a cut finger
to our mouth. Iron, irony—with both, don't we taste
the accident of ourselves? That curious
metallic twang: part sea, part bleeding stranger.

Translation

Despite the sweet plainness with which Jacqui sings
a kiss is just a kiss, it isn't. A kiss goes
in search of what a mouth needs and translates sadness
from one tongue to another. Like the poems

my son's class hated till a classmate, whose shaved
head rhymed with a backwards John Deere cap,
renamed the Nobel laureate who wrote them.
Not Czeslaw Milosz, the boy said, *Coleslaw Meatloaf.*

This mnemonic trick enough to get twenty-three mouths
hungrily around a Polish great grandfather of a poet.
All morning what they thought would taste flat
filled the classroom like takeout from an immigrant café.

All morning they found angels and angst, lost rivers
and Flemish still lifes worth a second helping.
Jacqui kisses me when I'm lost or distracted, when even
my shadow is off duty. I kiss back till her mouth

changes into song or forgiveness. Or some throaty
darkness I never thought to taste. Poems revise us
the way kisses make us repent of who we thought we were.
Translate me again. I have years and seconds.

Between

A newborn curled between us, we replot desire
The slow thinking we do with our flesh
Her hunger wakes you which in turn wakes me
To fields multiplied by crickets and déjà vu

The slow thinking we do with our flesh
Opens new rooms but how do we find our way
To fields multiplied by crickets and déjà vu
Her mouth invents a grammar of waiting

Opens new rooms but how do we find our way
My thumb your finger my finger your hair
Her mouth invents a grammar of waiting
Our pasts fanning out across hedge and lawn

My thumb your finger my finger your hair
As if open windows and touching could translate
Our pasts fanning out across hedge and lawn
Why is falling asleep mostly about falling

As if open windows and touching could translate
When you when I when the room spins darkly
Why is falling asleep mostly about falling
Go slowly love, trace the backs of these hands

When you when I when the room spins darkly
Her hunger wakes you which in turn wakes me
Go slowly love, trace the backs of these hands
We replot desire, a newborn curled between us

Moji

I like it, this *moji*, this pen name, this crayon signifier
coined by my three-year-old,
who signs his scribbles like a dyslexic angel.
I like it for its *mojo*,
which voodoo scribes breathe in
and cranky blues divas belt out.
For the way it marries *Mo* and *Genji*,
as if the Three Stooges had fallen
from another weekend pie fight into the plush
ritual of a tenth-century Japanese court.
For the way it burns like *mojave*
when I say it, but ends with a three-story *i*,
a Giacometti stick figure
posing as guardian or lighthouse.
For the way its four letters,
sometimes transposed as *jimo* or *ojim*, float
from one crayon hex to the next,
anchoring where my son wants them to,
to his name, to crinkled paper, to alien
cats with beards diving into a sleeping green sun.

For Dylan Larsen

Want Song

Two musics washing over me, and morning asks,
which loneliness comes closest to the inky
chromatics inside you? How can I answer?
The cricket in the tarantula's cage
chirrs the next world.
Meanwhile, scraps of Chopin float
up the stairs on my wife's trilling fingers
which played me whole
worlds ago, last night, when *I* was buried in *we.*

Self Portrait, in Clinic Garden

To pass through a cathedral of honey locusts,
to be prayed over, in dialects,
with hundreds of shaky fingers.

All this before I have settled with my oncologist.
So many histories to unspool,
so many topiary deer to sweat my way past.

I count roses, happy that they have agreed
for now to remain stationary.
Then follow the clinic path to a door

of glare marked *Pull.* A command, yes,
but also an invitation? My face
floating on this side, a nun

with crutches and orange tennis shoes
descending on that side, the light
between us twisting like delicious snakes.

Outside the Metropolitan Museum of Art

So why *did* the pretzel vendor tender me a discount?
Was it because I asked how much before

fishing out my wallet? Did I appear half transfigured
after wandering halls of grieving Madonnas?

Or did he pity me, my salt-and-pepper tweed
more retro Idaho than retro Soho?

Just a regular Tuesday between lunch and a subway
token to Port Authority, between Presidents' Day

and the year of the Rat. *Buck fifty*, he said,
looking straight at my shaggy moustache,

a twin of his only redder. Then to the next guy,
Two dollars. Ah, to be chosen by a ruddy pretzel man.

Widows I Have Known

The first was a violinist, youngish and unshaved, who kept her
husband in a carved box beside her toaster. She opened it once
when I came collecting for the newspaper. Splinters of bone mostly,
a little ash. Which she honored by risking her own bones. Riding a
red moped without a helmet, jumping out of a Cessna over saffron
fields. And the way she played Vivaldi—as if doing finger exercises
with the stars.

The second widow we left in a clearing a few weekends after opening
day. A doe. I was fourteen. She came back to nuzzle the sagebrush
where we cleaned the buck she had been running with. We had
enough tags to shoot her too, but some wanted to save their bullets
for antlers.

Number three was a girl in Lima, a widow by temperament if not
circumstance. You should have seen her selling guinea pigs in the
market. She grew sadder with each bill she tucked inside her blouse.
How did I know she was a widow? A white streak in her hair, a streak
of vultures in the sky.

Four, sometimes I feel like a widow. Silly since I am married. Silly
since I am a man. Still, I sympathize with female praying mantises,
who eat their husbands after mating.

Finally, the widow my daughter drew in school—cowboy boots,
spurs, a candelabra hat, and twins inside her. *So she won't be lonely,*
my daughter said. *You see, her husband got killed. At the rodeo.* You
mean he was gored? *No, I mean he fell from the flag pole, singing. Like
this, boom. With dark yellow hair. Flowers grew from his cuts. It was fast
fast fast. No one could save him, not even the clowns.*

To a Souvenir Mermaid

Poor girl—carved from a fence post in Cancun,
with a face more Pancho Villa than siren.
Your mouth is a study in late food poisoning
or early voodoo. Your painted lashes
could pass as centipede legs.
I have hung you above my study door as a reprieve.
One grows tired of always being seduced
by beauty. Besides, it's bracing to walk
under your strangler's hands,
to rub your splintery tail and think,
along with Byron, *We're a sad jar of atoms.*
Last night when I rolled over
my wife's Spanish dictionary, she asked,
when does *granada* mean pomegranate
and when does it mean hand grenade?
Never mind that I was trying to kiss her,
never mind that I hadn't been conjugated in weeks.
Noun and body—how both quiver
to be translated. Each time I touch you,
Sister, a briny sentence I didn't intend
tries to compose me. Souvenirs, like lovers,
sing us back to those places that were never ours.

To My Old Clothes

Where are you, togs of my past, huaraches and bow ties,
dickies and argyles, and the cracked
bowling shoes I christened Lazarus I and II?
Suppose a skylight opened in my closet,
and in you poured instead of stars.
Would you nibble my nakedness
like a school of kissing fish, or pull me under
with bad fashion? If old dreams
are gossamer, you are double-stitched ghosts,
binding me to histories that bear my secret
initials. Peacoats and fedoras from Salvation Army.
Jacquard smoking jacket. The rust leisure suit
I threw up in at prom. The floral sheet I wore
like a life sentence the Christmas
I contracted mono. And summer careers—
grease monkey, umpire, dog catcher, cook.
Not to mention the rococo ensembles I put on
and shrugged off in the name of conjugal love.
Do a few of you survive? Is there a Platonic shirtness
circling the earth, whose ether carries the musky
imprint of my torso? Did my Levis make it
to the Kremlin? Did even one faded bandanna,
baled and Goodwilled south, soak up the ardor
of Argentine soccer, Chilean poems?
I call you back, estranged ones. Each of you,
a funhouse mirror, a few of you, novellas.
Plot again for me those worlds I thought I outgrew.

IV. Stations of the Sky

Funeral Buffet

Blasphemous I know to fill my plate
    while the dead mumble about eternity.
If only I dared to peek in the casket,
    if only I could confess
to a priest who grasped the ontology of hunger.

The table stretches, long and lacquered
    as a bowling lane, full as a king's pantry,
and I always arrive famished.
    If only I knew how I lost my shoes
and who fitted me with this embossed silverware.

Such obscene abundance—quiche, figs, borsch,
    game hens stuffed with giblets
and all the vices of the overfed. If only I knew
    these great aunts buttoned up the back
like dogma, if only the croissants didn't glisten so.

Listen, dark cousin, avatar, or whoever you are—
    I'm famished with waiting,
full of this world and its pottage.
    When will you break bread with me,
lead me across the water, let me use your face

as a mirror? If only the dead could bury
    the dead, if flutes and peasant dancers
if a proper manual, if my unclean lips
    and a little rain. If eating
weren't a substitute for something else.

Trust

It was after the pot roast and home-made bread
but before we carried revised maps of kinship
to the highway. After my mother explained
the dying and dollars behind the family trust
but before the porch lights froze our kids
in shouts of *olley-olley-oxen free*. Two aging parents,
four adult siblings, and a forsythia blooming
at the window—pleasant enough to drive past once,

my mother said, but too damn yellow to look at
all morning. Three months after my father's
colonectomy, two weeks before more surgery.
After the dibsing, which my parents had insisted on,
but before we divided the burial plots. Something
shifted. A pause between stiff questions
and multiple-choice evasions, a smell well past
spring, a bruised color this side of final signatures.

We tried to sip at it or cough it away, but it wasn't
till my father tossed in a ritual sweatshirt story
that we relaxed. The one thing he valued
the fall of 1964, a hooded red sweatshirt,
which according to legend my mother bleached
accidentally on purpose to get it out of his closet.
Or cut into squares for a PTA quilt. Or buried
my sister's rabbit in. Or donated to needy Eskimos.

Or, in today's yarn, gave away to a pair
of Siamese twins on a scavenger hunt asking
for *something dead or something red*. Faded
but comfortable, it hovered over my parents' marriage,
like remembered passion, or a sleepy guardian
angel. And we rolled our shoulders to feel it,
that garment, and pulled the hood strings,
and breathed the musty cotton, half rag, half mantle.

Rehearsal

Either the wall is dripping eighth notes, or sugar ants
are trafficking again in borrowed sweetness.

Still hot, still the same in-between hour but morning
has slipped its tethers to nose around inside me.

I'm half breaths away from discovering holiness—
or pity. That shuttered bedroom I've carried since birth

and inside a luminous body waiting to be kissed
awake. The house natters on about permanence.

The responsible mail truck rumbles closer, then idles
down, making a ritual out of getting my name

wrong. Ants wait by walking. I kneel. If I were
my daughter, I'd hang my hair till it swept the floor.

1969

It was religion to me it was hiss and repeat
Pronouncing s's to a mirror in speech therapy
Six sleek swans swim swiftly southwards
Meanwhile my brother dreamed Vietnam in fire

Pronouncing s's to a mirror in speech therapy
I learned the sweet release of mouthing the world
Meanwhile my brother dreamed Vietnam in fire
NASA dreamed the moon the moon dreamed us

I learned the sweet release of mouthing the world
You'd think I was waiting for Lucy in the Sky
NASA dreamed the moon the moon dreamed us
I wanted to slip through words to the other side

You'd think I was waiting for Lucy in the Sky
To fix my mouth and unscramble my s's
I wanted to slip through words to the other side
In the shallows I patted Noreena the retarded girl

To fix my mouth and unscramble my s's
I swam wondering if my hair would turn green
In the shallows I patted Noreena the retarded girl
Never she said let them take away your secret name

I swam wondering if my hair would turn green
Six sleek swans swim swiftly southwards
Never she said let them take away your secret name
It was hiss and repeat it was religion to me

Chronos

Can there be an *after*, after Time gives up the ghost?
In those last moments, fat Victorian novels will auction
off their plots to the dumbest bidders. Clocks
will self-combust, and kitchen calendars will erupt
in a confetti of holy days and forgotten trysts.

But suppose one stray cell in each of us misfired,
and Time started ticking in our chests again? Soon
the old suffering would ooze back, everything smeared
with longing. Scented candles and gramophones,
codex of collarbone, crocuses huddled like saints.

Remember the pageants of desire we dreamed in church
pews behind a pair of bare shoulders? Remember
jealousy? Ah, bring back the pathos of the tattooist's
ink, oozy in its vials, poised forever between rose
and fiery dragon. How did we stand it—limping

into the next hour, stupid with hunger, wearing clothes
that didn't fit? Trying to balance the sadness
ledgers by staring at skuddy storm clouds. Such exquisite
lostness, waiting to be taken in by a late thaw,
waiting to be alphabetized by time line and trauma.

The Shapes Sadness Can Take

A boy on his back staring past smokestacks
wants the one white cloud to look like the state

where his father was born, then the town
that swallowed his mother following the divorce,

but the cloud wants only to resemble what passed
through it once. Not a jet which is a knife

tricked out with speed. But a flock of wrens,
one body and many, a floating room filled

with air and algorithms and crooked weather,
a forgiveness of wings, like God thinking.

Santiago Commute

I thought the trip was about catching the right *expreso*
and paying as you go. Forty-five minutes
from piano lesson to *pensión*.
Add a cloud of goat hairs if I stopped to pet *Diablo*,
the three-legged nanny. Add rain
to re-live each averted crash, each toothless man
selling himself a caramel at a time.
I got on the bus as a gringo exchange student
and stepped off as a story problem
waiting to be solved. Everything was exchange.
I traded baseball for soccer, hot dogs
for empanadas, smugness for faith.
If there were pesos to count,
I used the ten prostitutes at the ends of my hands.
If streets begged to be remembered,
I wiggled the ten nuns stuffed inside my shoes.
Forty pesos to a dollar,
a hundred dollars to keep me boarded and roomed,
one room in Santiago, Chile to translate
me into Spanish the year I turned seventeen.
At the slaughterhouse, trotters went in whole
and came out viscera tossed into a pickup.
At *El Estadio Nacional* where dissidents
once lay down to be shot, soccer gods
now zigzagged the field—part Pelé, part Orpheus.
I climbed on, I climbed off,
and in between, that bus had its way with me.
A charm dipped in pigeon blood pinned

to a baby's bib. Teenage girls bibbed
in blue uniforms giggling as they squeezed past.
The charm kept off my evil eye,
the giggling kept it guessing.
And the rain came down, and the Andes
rose up, and each dead dog grew wiser with decay.
Pointing from gutter to cathedral
to the clouds where ghost mongrels do their best running.
I chewed gum, sometimes caramels.
I chewed my shirt sleeve.
Miracles were everyday. Not the body
I got on the bus with, but the sacred
dirty air and tin saints that dreamed me as I stepped off.

Palimpsest

Twenty years those magenta lips have floated
above my head—heavy as grace,
graceful as sky writing. They float
centimeters above my two-fisted backhand
and winged-out hair and the tennis match
I'm busy losing on page 216 of my high school yearbook.

Which is to say, they float somewhere
between practical joke and dare,
whatever it was that led some anonymous lovely
to swipe what wasn't hers and kiss
my future. And this poem. Which also floats—
suspended between my line breaks

and your willingness to entertain pieces of yourself,
lonely reader. Has midnight ever peeled
you the way a cabaret dancer takes off
a sequined glove? Did you ever blow out
candles that left you in a delicious
darkness you hoped would nibble you clean?

That's how those lips hover, all whorls
and crenulations. A spaceship in search of an abductee,
a lipstick nimbus blessing whatever it passes
over—a boy leaning hard into the x and y
of next week's weather, which like
the tennis ball he's about to whack never arrives.

Birth Penny, Found
While Hoeing Cucumbers

I hope this penny fell into its grave the year
    it was minted, 1961, flung by the widow next door—
        an offering in behalf of the striped pajamas
    she lifted to the moon each night, then plumped
into the shape of a desiring husband.
    I hope this penny has cankered in my honor,
        that worms and star-nosed moles
    have woven a spell around it and chosen me
for a simpler sweatier life, of no insurance
    or birth control. I hope if I re-bury this penny,
        exactly at sundown, its *SF* mintage will mend
    itself into a *D*, since Denver is where I was conceived,
perhaps in an overgrown backyard like this,
    but probably in the trailer on cinder blocks
        my parents rented for $37 a month, under the GI bill.
    I hope Mr. Lincoln likes being scratched clean
with my broken thumbnail, though I've never
    cared for his one-cent profile, beard too stern,
        and no hat. And I hope the pilot passing
    over just now will wonder why some dolt
would kneel on the edge of a burned lawn, late morning,
    in the middle of his life. Sweet kingdom of leaves,
        peaches ripening, grasshoppers perfecting dizzy hops.

Austin Shuffle

What started as an imitation of a shell-shocked vet
ended in homage, a broken-leg shuffle
we parlayed into a dance step. Think the Zombie.
Think the Robot, infused with spastic cool.
Do the Austin—yeah yeah yeah. We Austined
at the bus stop, in the hall, during 3-on-3 pick up games.
And sometimes at lunch we'd sneak over

to watch Austin set up in front of the Odd Fellows
or Five Corners Tavern. He'd swing
down his knapsack, so heavy you'd swear
he'd been shoplifting car batteries. But no—
a typewriter, one of those monster Remingtons.
Then out came the tennis ball can, onion skin paper
rolled up inside like maps to lost mines.

We tossed loose change into the Dodgers cap
he used as a collection plate, and someone
with a minute hand counted down. Sixty seconds—
his fingers racing an invisible dictionary, head swinging
like an orangutan's. That Remington snared
street names and ad jingles, nursery rhymes
and communiques from the id. *5-4-3-2-1-Time.*

Austin lifted his hands, as if he had just finished
a concerto or autopsy. Then pulled out
a paragraph of bees. And dignity owned his eyes
and Five Corners owned the crumbly sidewalk
and the gutter owned the rain that failed
to wash anything clean. He scribbled 103 / 3 / Austin.
Words divided by errors divided by blankness.

Then he'd hand over his dispatch, so thin
you could see through it. And from that day
it owned you, whether you burned it
or chewed it or let ants carry it word by word
into the underworld. How to curse Uncle Sam
and shake the sky, how to hump sadness,
how to bathe in a shoe and polish your dirty wings.

The Dead Praying for Me

I have felt the dead praying for me, felt them drawing
their wispy ends over me, nightgowns
soaked with dew. Once in an empty
grocery aisle at noon, three times on a bus
so full of sips and sighs I never wanted to step off.

Perhaps it was a pair of sisters, recently drowned,
using my lost ATM card as a Ouija board,
or a dead mother who found an open channel
to me while seeking her derelict son.
A chance encounter refracted. No, inflected—

a catch in the air, a candle burning backwards,
then hands gentling me from inside.
Hands dropping a bucket
into my well, hands pulling back the ivy
to trace initials scratched there before I was born.

Questions for My Daemon

When my hand closes on lake water or humus,
when my eyes open under a field of stars, is it you I feel
humming inside me? Shall I carve you a mouth,
so you can play the sage ventriloquist,
or do you speak by not speaking? Shall I assign
you a historian's grasp of *horror vacui*, Gnosticism,
and tulip mania to help me believe in the past?

Listen, my lostness some afternoons makes me
think you've left me to settle in the ear
of some half-lame Appaloosa grazing the pasture.
If so, will any of the old tricks bring you back—
an open window, candles, a nonsense word
repeated until the house I'm sitting in sits
inside me? Last week, when the neighbor boy

borrowed a bicycle and pedaled five miles
up the canyon to end his life in a favorite grove,
where was his daemon? Did his devotion
to the gossip of quakies make him holy
or only sentimental? When he pulled
the trigger was he more naked or less?
Is it wrong to hold a soft spot for phrenology—

thirty-seven rooms in one haunted belfry
and a numbered illustration to help me stand
quietly in each? I keep confusing *ascetic*
and *aesthetic*. Does the song of the spheres
ever feature a gypsy band improvising the torpor
of twilight on stolen guitars? Why does *Antipodes*
make me feel I'm both leaving and being called home?

Bodies, Terrestrial

The poem wants hurt the way a flock of pigeons
wants to imitate the Holy Ghost,
the way blood leaking
from a body in an alley wants
to resemble the outlines of Wisconsin.
Without sufficient hurt, we are better off
trimming rose bushes or washing
dirty linen. Think of hurt
as a transaction between your body and someone else's.

A slap, a punch, a pencil stabbed into the thigh—
these hurt like a newborn opening its eyes.
History hurts more slowly,
like fog or an army marching, like mercury
in a river licking two shores at once.
Words let us poison
a small room without getting out of our chair.
Hurt reads the entire dictionary
and can translate from Aramaic to Zulu.

The poem would like to convert hurt from stabs
and tremors to earth tones,
but not everyone agrees on the colors of hurt.
Hurt fills the infinite blue.
Lucky for us, we are leaky tea cups.
When morning, with its raffle of trees
and burnt umber,
hurts us out of sleep, we fly up.
What falls, rain. What falls through us, dé jà vu.

After, we home to our bodies like a thumb
to the thumb sucker's mouth.
Some of us resemble wind socks,
some, cemeteries storing decades of hurt.
When someone drips hurt
on us, or lets it pool at our feet,
we sigh God's name. Not the whole hurt,
but as many vowels,
as much of His body as will fit in one mouth.

Vineyard

Yes, the zucchinis grow heavy and wicked,
and yes, a porcupine parses the orchard
one rummy apple at a time.
But the true inventory begins when two boys
in mummy bags carve up Cassiopeia,
first with index fingers, then with closed eyes
and a buried love of their mothers, expressed as sleep.

Next the bicycle hanging on the porch pedals
backwards, a poor man's time machine.
Which means it's time
for the zephyr and the uncle smoking
a hand-rolled cigarette
under the eaves to trade places.
Prepare then to say hello to wind tucked

into scuffed boots, to salute a laid-off longshoreman
pushing clouds across the lake.
Meanwhile, a croquet hoop and an ax
in the peonies create
a cautionary tale by moonlight,
whose heroine huddles in the front room
trying to free Chopin from torn sheet music.

Beneath her, in the bathroom, her older sister urinates
on a plastic wand that turns
her misgivings the shade of her boyfriend's car.
To the side of the house,
a salamander in a bucket holds the night
ransom. Up ahead, one peach tree, three grafts,
like agony buried in Jesus and the two thieves.

The Father who suffered him to be nailed
climbs over the fence. Wanders his overgrown
vineyard in an underfed body, to remember
lostness. Takes a swig of syrupy Coke
left out all day, coughs once, then wipes
his mouth on the neck of a sleeping mastiff,
who dreams apocalypse in greens and terrible blues.

Acknowledgments

Special thanks to the editors of the following magazines and journals, in which the following poems, sometimes under different titles, first appeared:

Agni: "Widows I Have Known"
Antioch Review: "Not Pastoral"
Barrow Street: "Walking on My Hands, Hotel Pool"
Chariton Review: "Planaria"
Crazyhorse: "Santiago Commute"
Field: "Funeral Buffet"
"Good Friday"
"Legion"
"Yellowstone, Burning"

Gulf Coast: "Want Song"
Grand Street: "Landscape, with Hungry Gulls"
Image: "This World, Not the Next"
Many Mountains Moving: "Translation"
Michigan Quarterly Review: "On Thawing Her Milk"
Mid-American Review: "Salamander"
New England Review: "Moji"
New York Review of Books: "Rehearsal"
Nimrod: "Black Box"
"Drainage Pipe Under I-89"
Paris Review: "Vineyard"
"Winter Takeout"
Poetry Northwest: "Spider Luck"
Quarterly West: "Allegory, with Famous Poet"
"Birth Penny, Found While
Hoeing Cucumbers"
"The Dead Praying for Me"
"The Shapes Sadness Can Take"
River Styx: "Chronos"
"Self Portrait in Clinic Garden"
"To A Souvenir Mermaid"
Runes: "Tarantula on the Back of My Wrist"
Salmagundi: "Questions for My Daimon"

Southern Review:	"By Road and Sky"
	"On Being Asked, *Have you ever*
	written about Jacqui's paintings?"
Tampa Review:	"Hand Poem"
	"On a Thumbprint in a Library Book"
	"Platonic"
Tar River Poetry:	"Austin Shuffle"
	"House Sit"
	"Infinity Hopscotch"
	"Outside the Metropolitan Museum of Art"
Threepenny Review:	"Landscape for Several Pairs of Hands"
	"Trust"
Times Literary Supplement:	"Old Masters"
Western Humanities Review:	"Between"
	"Cottage Industry"
	"Palimpsest"
	"To My Old Clothes"

"Landscape, with Hungry Gulls" was republished in *The Pushcart Prize 2005*; "Moji" made an appearance in *Poetry Daily*; and the following poems were posted on the Joseph Campbell Corner website (Sara Lawrence): "By Road and Sky," "Good Friday," "Infinity Hopscotch," "Landscape for Several Pairs of Hands," "Landscape, with Hungry Gulls," "Platonic," "Spider Luck," and "Vineyard."

I am indebted to the BYU College of Humanities, the Sewanee Writers' Conference, and the Utah Arts Council for support that made this collection possible.

Thanks to Richard Mathews at University of Tampa Press for his unflagging goodwill. And thanks to Leslie Norris, Natasha Saje, Jim Barnes, Lola Haskins, and Timothy Liu, for their scrutiny and encouragement. Thanks as well to Charlie Scott for lending me his Coleslaw Meatloaf anecdote in "Translation."

I especially want to acknowledge fellow travelers Shannon Castleton, Dennis Clark, Gina Clark, Steven Graves, Scott Hatch, Susan Howe, Kimberly Johnson, John Talbot, and Sally Taylor, with whom I regularly broke bread. Finally, love and affection to Jacqui, my first reader always.

About the Author and the Artist

Lance Larsen is the winner of the 2004 Tampa Review Prize for Poetry. His first book, *Erasable Walls,* was published in 1998 by New Issues, and his poems have appeared in *New Y ork Review of Books, Paris Review, Kenyon Review, New Republic, Threepenny Review, Southern Review, The Times Literary Supplement,* and elsewhere. He holds a Ph.D. from the University of Houston and has received several other awards, including a Pushcart Prize and fellowships from Sewanee, Writers at Work, and the Cultural Arts Council of Houston. Director of English Graduate Studies at Brigham Young University, he is married to painter and mixed-media artist Jacqui Larsen.

Jacqui Larsen has shown her work in New York, Illinois, Texas, Utah, California, and at the Millennium Arts Center in Washington, D.C. The recipient of numerous grants, awards, and fellowships, she uses found text, patterns and images in both her collages and paintings. Her work can be seen online at www.newvisionart.com

About the Book

In All Their Animal Brilliance is set in Adobe Garamond Pro types based on the roman types of Claude Garamond and the italic types of Robert Granjon. First cast as metal types in the sixteenth century, these enduring letterforms, both readable and elegant, have been beautifully rendered in digital form. The book was designed and typeset by Richard Mathews at the University of Tampa Press. It has been printed on acid-free recycled Glatfelter Natures Natural text paper in support of the Green Press Initiative by Thomson-Shore of Dexter, Michigan.

Poetry from the University of Tampa Press

Jenny Browne, *At Once*

Richard Chess, *Chair in the Desert*

Richard Chess, *Tekiah*

Kathleen Jesme, *Fire Eater*

Lance Larsen, *In All Their Animal Brilliance**

Julia B. Levine, *Ask**

Sarah Maclay, *Whore**

John Willis Menard, *Lays in Summer Lands*

Jordan Smith, *For Appearances**

Lisa M. Steinman, *Carslaw's Sequences*

Richard Terrill, *Coming Late to Rachmaninoff*

* Denotes winner of the Tampa Review Prize for Poetry